Two lectures, on the natural history of the Caucasian and Negro races.

Josiah Clark Nott

TWO LECTURES,

ON THE

NATURAL HISTORY

OF THE

CAUCASIAN AND NEGRO RACES,

BY

JOSIAH C. NOTT M D

Si ma raison vient d en haut c'est la voix de quelqu'une perh p r
elle, il faut que je l'ecoute

MOBILE.
PRINTED BY DADE AND THOMPSON

1844.

PREFACE

With the view of exciting a taste for literary and scientific pursuits, several gentlemen proposed a course of *popular* Lectures in Mobile, leaving the choice of subjects to those gentlemen who might be disposed to embark in the enterprise.

Amongst others I was solicited to take part, and the following pages contain two lectures which I delivered with some modification in the Introduction, and the addition of an Appendix.

These lectures were written in the midst of pressing professional engagements, without the most distant idea of publication, and I have since their delivery, been so much occupied that I have not had time to copy the manuscript, or superintend properly the printing. They will therefore be found full of typographical errors, errors in style, punctuation &c.— Parts of my lectures, however, have been misunderstood and misrepresented, and I have therefore determined to publish without delay, in self-defence.

We have no good library in Mobile, and those who know the extent and difficulty of my subject, need not be told that this is an ample reason for the omission of many important facts. I have drawn largely from the able works of Pritchard, Caldwell, Gliddon, Morton, and others whose quotations and facts can be relied on.

The parts which treat of the effect of crossing races, are those to which I wish to draw more particular attention, as these facts have not heretofore been sufficiently considered.

Mobile, Feb., 1, 1844.

INTRODUCTION

The question of the unity of the Human Race is a grave one—it has elicited a vast deal of talent and research, and is deserving of the profoundest study—most candid men have acknowledged its difficulty, and that all past time has afforded no data, by which it can be definitively settled. My object is to place before the world new facts, which may assist in forming a rational conclusion on this vexed question.

When we look around us and see the various complexions and various physical conformations which exist in the human race, as the Caucasian, Mongol, Malay, Indian and Negro, we have naturally forced upon our minds the inquiry, *are these derived from one pair, or are they of distinct origins?*

This subject is attended by the same difficulty which has impeded the advancement of other departments of Natural History, as well as the Sciences of Astronomy and Geology. In their infancy, discoveries in these sciences, were regarded as inconsistent with the Mosaic account of the creation, and have encountered determined opposition from well meaning and other religious persons. The scientific men who have been bold enough to speak truth, and to uphold the works of God, have been persecuted by those who mistake their own intellects for the measure of wisdom, and their own passions and prejudices for the will of heaven.

When Galileo promulgated the great truth, that the sun stands still, and the earth moves round it, he was attacked and persecuted by the whole priesthood—he was twice brought before the Inquisition and forced to renounce his doctrines—Time, however, has served to show, that Galileo was right, and the Bible still stands "the rock of ages."

The Unity of the Human Race is a question appertaining to Natural History, which should be left open to free and honest investigation, and made to stand or fall according to the facts.

I should therefore, have much preferred, not to involve theological points, but I know that *others* will do it—that I shall have anathemas heaped on my head, and wrong motives imputed to me—false issues will be made and the true points for discussion evaded.

I am prepared for all this—those who know me well, I have the vanity to believe, will do me justice, and I am quite indifferent to the censure of those who hold up Christ as their model, while they are pouring out phials of wrath

1

My object is truth, and I care not which way the question is decided, provided the decision is a correct one. I have accumulated a number of curious and interesting facts, some of which are new, and I have interpreted them dispassionately. My conclusions may be disputed, but they cannot be disproved in the present state of the science of Natural History.—*New facts* must be brought to light before *certain* conclusions to the contrary are arrived at.

The Mosaic account, as will be seen in my appendix, sheds no satisfactory light on this question. The book of Genesis has proved to be a field of endless and angry discussion amongst Doctors of Divinity and they are now no nearer agreeing than they were 2000 years ago. *All that they have proved, is, that they know nothing about it.* The world was made for us all, and there is no reason why I am not as much entitled to an opinion as my Protestant, Jew or Catholic.

Luther, speaking of the Book of Genesis says "There has not hitherto been any one in the church, that has with sufficient propriety and exactness, expounded the whole of these subjects for expositors have so mixed them up with various, diversified and never ending inquiries, as to make it apparent *that God has reserved to himself alone, this majesty of wisdom, and the sound understanding of this chapter,* leaving to us the general knowledge that the world had a beginning, and was created out of nothing by God. This general knowledge is clearly derived from the text. But with respect to the particular things, there is very much that is involved in difficulty and doubt, and about which questions without end are agitated.

Calvin says "Two opposite errors are common—some persons finding that themselves or the bulk of men have been imposed upon, reject in the mass all religious doctrines, others with weak credulity, indiscriminately embrace whatsoever is proposed to them in the name of God. Each extreme is wrong. The former class filled with proud prejudice, bar themselves out from the way of improvement, the others rashly expose themselves to every wind of error. From these two extremes, Paul recalls the Thesalonians to the middle path, *forbidding the condemnation of any sentiment till it be first examined* and admonishing that we should exercise a just judgment before we receive as certain, that which is proposed to us. *Nothing is more hurtful than the petulent and conceited disposition, by which we take up a dislike to any sentiment, without taking the trouble of a fair examination.*"

When the Doctors differ, who is to decide? My reply is

God himself. We are to appeal to Analogies, facts, induction and to the universal and undeviating laws of Nature.— *The plurality of species in the human race does no more violence to the Bible, than do the admitted facts of Astronomy and Geology.*

Astronomy has struggled through all opposition. Geology and Natural History, though still under the ban of the inquisition, are rapidly progressing towards perfection. The religion of Christ too, is advancing as the world becomes more enlightened, and they can and will march on together, receiving light from each other, and upholding the wisdom, goodness and glory of God.

The study of Natural Theology is receiving more and more attention every year, and my firm conviction is, that great injury has been done to revealed religion by forbidding the study of God in the vastness and majesty of his works. This is the study by which the existence of a God is demonstrated, and when this first step is gained, the next which the enquirer takes, is to ask if God has spoken to man? If so, when and where?

"How do you know," said a traveller to a poor Arab of the desert, 'that there is a God?" "In the same manner,' he replied, "that I trace the footsteps of an animal by the prints which it leaves upon the sand.'

The words and works of God, if *properly understood*, can never be opposed to each other—they are two streams which flow from the same pure fountain, and must at last mingle in the great sea of truth.

In my lectures I distinctly and honestly disclaimed any wish or intention of throwing doubts over the divine origin of either the New or Old Testaments, and went on to say, "Take away even the Divinity of the Bible, and he is no friend to man who would wish to pull the fabric down—it is necessary for our welfare in this world, that good morals should be taught, and where, I would ask, can we find a system so pure and so conducive to our happiness as that of Christ?"

It should be born in mind, that we are now in the 19th century, which is marked by an advanced state of the sciences hitherto unknown, and that Biblical commentators have been *forced to make large concessions to Astronomy, Natural History and Geology.*

There is another important point to be remembered in this discussion, and I refer to my appendix for illustration. The Rev. John Pye Smith, D. D., says that "to those who have studied the phraseology of scripture, there is no rule of inter position more certain than this, that universal terms are often used to signify only *a very large* amount in number, or quantity. Dr. George Young, says that "*all, every one, the whole* and such like expressions, are very often used to denote *a great many, or a large proportion*"*

Now why I would ask, does not this apply to what is said of the human race, as well as to any thing else?

D. Smith says, "that it is certain the Hebrews (though so long time under the instruction and guidance of Moses) were ignorant of the spheroidal shape of the globe." And it is more than probable that this fact, as well as many others of Geographical and scientific character *were not revealed to Moses*. The same remark applies to St. Paul and the other writers of the New Testament, they did not pretend to have fathomed all the mysteries of the Almighty, and we have no reason to suppose they knew any thing of the interior of Africa or of the existence of America. The unity of the human race is spoken of so seldom in the New Testament, and in such a passing way as to leave room for rational doubts on the subject. We are therefore at liberty to appeal to facts.

I will here lay down a chain of propositions for examination, and I would appeal to every candid man who has studied Geology and Natural History, to say whether they are not true.

1st. Have there not been *several* creations and destructions in the Animal and Vegetable kingdoms, *previous* to the creation spoken of by Moses?

2nd. Is it not admitted by Naturalists, that many of the animals *now* upon the earth are entirely different from those which existed *before* the flood, and that if the flood was universal these animals *have been created since*?

3d. Is it not admitted by Naturalists that the Ark only contained the animals which *inhabited the part of the earth in which Noah dwelt*, and that it is a Zoological and physical impossibility that the Ark could have contained pairs and septuples of *all* the animals now on the earth?

4th. Is it not a fact, that Islands newly emerged from the

<hr/>

Note.— Again the devil taketh him (Jesus) up into an exceeding high mountain and showeth him *all the kingdoms of the world* and the glory of them.

And the devil taking him up into an high mountain, showed unto him all the kingdoms of the world in a moment of time.

Now a *strict construction* of these passages would lead to the inference that St. Matthew, St. Luke and others were ignorant of the spheroidal shape of the globe as were the Hebrews, but it will be seen in the appendix, that such constructions should not always be given.

ocean, become covered with plants, *differing from all others* in other parts of the globe—thus showing that the creative power of the Almighty is *still* exercised, whenever circumstances are ready for it?

5th. Does not all this prove that the account given by Moses is *imperfect*, and that much has been *omitted* of the infinite works of the creator, both *before* and *after* the creation of which he speaks?

6th Has God any where said that he never intended to create another man, or that other races were not created in distant parts of the globe. I would ask, after all these admitted truths, is there any thing so revolting in the idea that a Negro, Indian, or Malay, may have been created since the flood of Noah, or (if the flood was not universal) before this epoch?

I know it will be said that Negroes existed at the time that Moses wrote, but to this I will reply that Moses must have known equally well of a vast number of animals which did not descend from the Ark, and which were not included in his account.

I set out then with the proposition, that there is a Genus, Man, comprising two or more species—that physical causes cannot change a White man into a Negro, and that to say this change has been effected by a direct act of providence, is an assumption which *cannot be proven, and is contrary to the great chain of Nature's law.*

LECTURE I.

Before entering upon the Natural History of the human race, it is indispensably necessary, as a preliminary step, to examine some points in chronology, and to take a glance at the early history of Egypt. I must show that the Caucasian or White and the Negro races were distinct at a very remote time, and *that the Egyptians were Caucasians.* Unless this point can be established the contest must be abandoned.

In order to show how completely we are left in the dark on this subject by the Old Testament, it will be necessary to make some allusion to the *diversity* of chronological computations.

The commonly received opinion is that our globe was created 4004 years before Christ, and that the Deluge took place 2348 B C.

These computations, let it be remembered, were made by Archbishop Usher, were adopted by an Act of the British Parliament, and are the dates annexed to our Bibles.

Now no one will pretend that Arch Bishop Usher was inspired, nor that his date have not been other divines as learned as himself—still less will any one pretend that the British Parliament is distinguished either for inspiration or piety.— These dates then are entitled to no more respect than are the received opinions.

Some may be surprised to learn that there are, besides that of Bishop Usher, *more than 300 computations,* for the creation and deluge—these computations too are made by learned divines and differ at least 1500 years. I will cite a few only of the most prominent, as I am desirous of avoiding prolixity.

	Creation	Deluge		Exodus
Septuagint	5580 B C	3246 B C	Josephus,	1648 B C
Hebrew text	4161	2225	Eng Bible	1491
English Bible	4004	2348		

These are sufficient to show how widely the highest and most competent authorities differ on these points.

There is even a difference of 10 years in the dates given for the birth of Christ, and Moses has left no data, nor is there any thing in the History of Egypt, by which *His* time can be determined.

Modern science establishes beyond the possibility of a doubt, the fact, that these dates, for the creation at least, are too short, and probably by many thousand years. I presume there are few if any divines of the present day, conversant with Geology and Natural History, who do not concur in this opinion, and who do not believe there have been other floods besides the one spoken of by Moses.

In writing the Natural History of the human race, we must commence with the subsidence of *the* Deluge, this as I have stated, is placed by Usher, 2348 B C. Now I propose to show by positive proofs from recent examination of Egyptian monuments that this date is erroneous—that Negroes existed in Africa before this date of the flood, and that there is reason to believe they did not descend from Noah's family.

Moses dwelt in Egypt some 1500 years B C, and is said to have been learned in all the wisdom of this singular and interesting country. We have abundant account of the Pyramids, her magnificent temples, her obelisks and other monuments of her surprising greatness.

These monuments are embossed with hieroglyphics which have puzzled the brains of the most learned antiquaries for centuries, and strange to say, the hour of discovery of a key by which they could be deciphered, has remained so until ...

About twenty years ago, Champollion, who was sent to Egypt by the French Government, during his researches found the celebrated Rosetta stone, on which were engraved three inscriptions in different characters.

The 1st was composed of mere hieroglyphics—the 2nd was the Demotic, or common written language of Egypt and the 3d was Greek.

The event recorded on this stone was the coronation of Epiphanes &c, which took place at Memphis in March 196 B C, and the whole inscription would take up two ordinary or two pages.

On comparing the three different inscriptions, they were found to be exact translations of each other, and a key was thus at once furnished, by which most of the chronological mysteries of Egypt were to be unravelled. Since that time Egyptian hieroglyphics have been read and translated with almost as much ease as Greek or Hebrew.

We now know more of the history of Egypt prior to Moses,

than we do of the history of France or England, prior to Charlemangne or Alfred.

I am mainly indebted to Mr J. S Gliddon for the facts I shall use on this subject Mr. G lived in Egypt 23 years, is intelligent, well informed, and I learn from those who know him well, is an amiable and honorable gentleman.

A joint commission was sent to Egypt some years ago by the French Government, and the Grand Duke of Tuscany, headed by two of the most distinguished men of the age, Champollion and Rosellini, for the purpose of examining the monuments of this country. On their return home they each published works which have been the greatest literary wonders of the age

Mr. Gliddon, in addition to his opportunities of examining their works, has enjoyed their friendship and intimacy, and has travelled over the same ground they have and examined the monuments for himself

Now here are three gentlemen of character and competency, who have no object in teaching falsehoods, and when they state a fact as *certain* we *must believe them*—they must know more of these subjects than Oxford and Andover professors

Historians have assigned to Egypt 31 Dynasties, comprising 378 Kings, previous to the conquest by Alexander the great, which took place 332 B C , and a large proportion of these dynasties have been *verified* by the hieroglyphic inscriptions The obelisks, tombs and other monuments had inscribed on them the name of each monarch, the number of years he reigned, the principal events of his reign, &c., and by putting together these reigns in their proper order, we get at positive dates

The *positive* monumental data go back to the year B. C 2272, which is *within 72 years* of Usher's date of the flood.

The list of monuments are not *perfect* beyond that date— many have been destroyed, in consequence of which, the date of some of the Kings cannot be determined with precision.

Besides Manetho, the Egyptian historian, we have the authority of Herodotus, Eratosthenes, Diodorus, Josephus, the old Egyptian Chronicle, as well as the hieroglyphics, to prove that Menes was the first King of Egypt—it is certain that he reigned *long previous* to the positive date above given, and Champollion and Rosellini place him about 2750 years B. C *which is 400 years before our date of the deluge.*

The Pyramids were built between the time of Menes, the 1st King, and 2272 B. C , and hieroglyphic writing was common at the time of the Pyramids.

Now all these statements are not mere conjectures, but positive facts, engraven upon stone at the time the events recorded transpired, they are just as much to be relied on as the inscriptions on the Bunker Hill, or Battle Monument at Baltimore.

Another proof of the remote date of the flood, or of its limited extent, is seen in the great age of certain trees in Africa and Central America—distinguished Botanists assert that some of these trees are 6000 years old—full grown trees may have been created when Adam was, but we have no reason to believe they have been since—this fact then, which no Botanists doubts, proves that the flood took place at least 6000 years ago, or it was not universal.

It is recorded that the largest Pyramid took 100,000 men 20 years to build it, the immense masses of stone of which it is built, were brought from a great distance and transported across the Nile. And it is recorded in hieroglyphics, that it took 10 years to prepare the material before the construction commenced.

Now let me ask if several hundred of these pyramids existed, with a vast number of other stupendous monuments—at Memphis and Thebes were built and contained with the country around, a population which could execute all these wonderful things—if all the useful arts and sciences, together with Astronomy, existed at this remote date. How many centuries previous must this country have been populated? It is difficult for the mind to reach it. Reflect for a moment on the slow progress which a nation must make from infancy to such perfection.

The world has been most egregiously deceived by Greek and Roman historians—Herodotus particularly, who has been called the father of history, should with more propriety, be called the father of romance.

Herodotus was in Egypt about 430 B. C., during the dominion of the Persians, long after she had fallen from her pristine greatness. He was ignorant of the language, was looked upon like other foreigners, as an 'impure gentile'—did not associate with the higher castes, and received his information as other travellers, through ignorant and often dishonest interpreters. The same remarks apply with still greater force to Diodorus and other writers of later times. They were totally unable to decypher the hieroglyphics, and recorded vague traditions and stories of events 2 or 3000 years before their day.

Of what they saw with their own eyes, they may be

supposed to speak with some degree of accuracy—perhaps as much as would a Russian or Egyptian traveller in the U States.

Manetho is the historian most worthy of credit, as his dynasties and other facts are in accordance with the hieroglyphic inscriptions, which is not only the best test we could have at this late day, but a test which is almost conclusive.

Manetho was an Egyptian Priest, who lived B. C. about 260 years. He of course was familiar with the language and literature of his country, and as his history was written by the order of one of the Ptolemies, who was then on the throne, of course the Archives of the nation and all sources of information were thrown open to him. Hieroglyphic writing was then in use and he was familiar with it.

Unfortunately there is no copy of Manetho's works extant and we have only extracts from them in the works of Josephus and others. Next to a pure copy of the Bible, I know of no work so important as a correct and full copy of his writings—it is to be hoped that one may yet be discovered.

Egypt is the earliest point of civilization of which we have any records. The history of this country is doubly interesting to us as it has been asserted by most historians, it was originally inhabited by negroes, and that from this race all the Arts and Sciences have been derived.

I shall however, be able to show satisfactorily, that recent investigations have overthrown all previously received opinions on the subject, and that the Egyptians were a Caucasian race.

In the allotment of territories to the offspring of Noah, Egypt was given as an inheritance to Mizraim, the son of Ham. He must have proceeded with his companions from the banks of the Euphrates, along the borders of the Mediterranean, and across the Isthmus of Suez, to his point of destination—as lower Egypt, near the mouth of the Nile was most easy of access, and the most fertile country, it is reasonable to suppose that here their first settlement was made. Mizraim being a descendant of Noah, was of course a Caucasian.

Shem and Ham were twin brothers—the word Shem, means white and Ham, means dark, or swarthy, but not black. It is probably therefore, that there was the same difference between them, that we often see between brothers here. Many have supposed Ham to be the progenitor of the negro race. There was no curse upon him, and there is nothing in the Bible which induces such a belief, but this point is settled by the fact which I shall prove, that the Egyptians were not Negroes

The curse of heaven fell upon Canaan, but we have no reason to believe that the curse was a physical one. Canaan too, took possession of Palestine, and not any part of Africa and his descendants were Caucasians

Mr. J S Gliddon asserts that it can be proven by paintings and sculptures, of a date earlier than 1500 years B. C — that the Canaanites and Negroes were as different as the whites and negroes are of the present age, and that the negroes then presented the same physical characteristics which they do now after a lapse of 3,300 years

The drawings and sculptures of this early date, often represent negroes as slaves and captives, and as an evidence of the estimation in which this black race was held, even at this remote date, the inscriptions designated their country as *"barbarian, and their race as porters"*

You will remember that the Nile runs north and empties into the Mediteranean, and that it takes its rise towards the center of Africa, far into the country which is now, and has been, as far back as history can trace, inhabited by Negroes

According to most historians, civilization commenced high up the Nile in Ethopia, and was thence brought down towards its mouth into Egypt. Late investigations, however have disproved this assertion, and shown by positive facts, that the oldest monuments are found in Egypt, particularly at Memphis

It is now proven that time and circumstances did not effect any material change in Hams progeny, and that his lineal descendants were pure Caucasians. They very naturally were modified in upper Egypt, by admixture with the Ethopians Arabs and others, who bordered on their territory. To this day, Mr. Gliddon says, the Fellahs, or people of lower Egypt are but little mixed

Now I would ask with Mr. Gliddon, how long must it have taken for the descendants of Ham to have gone from the banks of the Euphrates in Asia, into Africa and up the Nile 1500 miles—there grow into a powerful nation—carry the Arts and Sciences to the highest state of perfection, and next, as an additional evidence of civilization, turn perfectly black—afterwards come down the Nile again 1500 miles to its mouth, and to cap the climax, turn white again this too, in a climate where no one's skin has changed in the last 1000 years! Now if there is any miracle in the Bible more wonderful than this, I should like to know what it is. All these events too, according

to the Hebrew version, happen in 100 years, and according
to the Septuagint 500

Besides the proofs drawn from the hieroglyphics, paintings,
sculptures, &c. there are others which not only strongly cor-
roborate, but amount to perfect demonstration of the fact, that
the Ancient Egyptians were Caucasians.

The great Naturalist Cuvier, has spent much time and la-
bor on this point, and after a careful examination of 50 Mum-
mies, asserts that they are Caucasian, and have no resemblance
whatever to the Negro the head, the whole skeleton and
the hair are Caucasian. In this opinion all distinguished naturalists concur.

Dr. Morton of Philadelphia, who has devoted much attention to these subjects, and who has acquired a distinguished
reputation, not only in this country, but throughout the Scientific world, has thrown very important light on this point.

Dr. Morton's facts are drawn from an examination of 100
Egyptian heads taken from 7 different repositories of the dead,
particularly Memphis and Thebes. These heads were collected and presented to him by Mr. Gliddon, who was Consul
at Cairo, for 23 years.

In a paper read by Dr. Morton before the American Philosophical Society, he first took a view of those nations with
whom the Egyptians appear to have held intercourse, either
for war or commerce in the early epochs of their history, and
amongst those whom he has been able to identify, from a comparison of the heads figured in the work of Rossellini, are
the Celts the Scythians, the Pelasgic and Semetic nations, the
Hindoos, Arabs and Negroes. He has classed the whole series of heads in the following manner

1st Arcto Egyptians—Under which designation are em-
braced the purer Caucasian nations as seen in the Semetic
tribes of Western Asia, and the Pelasgic communities of
Southern Europe

2d Austro-Egyptians—In which the cranium blends the
characters of the Hindoo and Southern Arab which people,
in the opinion of the author, were engrafted on the aboriginal
population of Ethopia, and thus gave rise to the celebrated
Meroite nations of antiquity

3d Negroloid crania, in which the osteological development
corresponds to that of the Negro, while the hair, though harsh
and sometimes wiery, is long and not wooly thus presenting
the combination of features which are familiar in the Malatto
grades of the present day

4th Negro

In many crania, the Arcto-Egyptian, Austro-Egyptian, and Semetic characters are variously blended, while a few also present traces of Negro lineage, modifying the features of the preceding types

The Caucasian Crania, in the whole, constitute 9 in 10, the Negroloid, about 1 in 11—and out of the whole 100 skulls, there is but one unmixed Negro.

A very striking fact too, is, that the pure Caucasian heads are found at Memphis, near the mouth of the Nile, and as you ascend the river into the interior of Africa and approach Nubia, the Caucasian character is gradually lost—they become mingled with Negro and other tribes

The author refers the blending of Arcto-Egyptian and Austral-Egyptian and other communities, to three principal periods of Egyptian history, viz

1st The conquest by the Hykshos or Shepherd Kings, 2082 B C, when the Egyptians of all ranks were driven into Ethiopia for a period of 260 years

2d The Ethiopian Dynasty of 3 Kings which lasted 40 years, beginning 719 years B C.

3d The conquest by Cambyses B C 525, when the distinctions of caste and nation were comparatively disregarded for upwards of two centuries during which period the people of Asia, Europe and Nigritia, were freely admitted into Egypt

Dr Morton's ethnographical researches, conjoined with the evidence of history and the monuments, have led him to draw the following conclusions

1st. That Egypt was originally peopled by the Caucasian race

2d That the great preponderance of heads, conforming in all their characters to those of the purer Caucasian nations, as seen in the Pelasgic and Semetic tribes, suggests the inference that the valley of the Nile derived its primitive civilized inhabitants from one of these sources, and that the greater proportion of this series of crania in Lower Egypt may, perhaps, serve to indicate the seats of early colonization

3d That the Austral-Egyptian, or Meroite communities, were in a great measure derived from the Indo-Arabian stock thus pointing to a triple Caucasian source for the origin of the Egyptians, when regarded as one people extending from Meroe to the Delta.

4th That the Negro race exists in the catacombs in the mixed or Negroloid character that even in this modified type their presence is comparatively unfrequent and that it Negroes, as is more than probable were numerous in Egypt, their social position was chiefly in ancient times what it yet is —that of Plebians, Servants and Slaves

Independent of the bearing of many of these interesting facts, the conclusion to my mind, is irresistable, that the civilization of Egypt is attributable to these Caucasian heads, because civilization does not now and never has as far as we know from history, been carried to this perfection by any other race than the Caucasian—how can any reasoning mind come to any other conclusion?

It is clear then that history, the Egyptian Monuments, her paintings and sculptures, the examination of skulls by Cuvier, Morton and others, Analogy, and every thing else connected with this country, combine to prove beyond the possibility of a doubt, that the Ancient Egyptian race were Caucasians

Positive historical facts prove too, that Egypt has been conquered in early times by various inferior tribes, and the blood of her people adulterated Besides the conquest of the Hykshos, the Ethiopians, Persians and others, she has more recently been conquered by the Greeks, the Romans and Turks

But even the pure blood of Greece and Rome could not wash out the black stain, both moral and physical, which she has received.

Naturalists have strangely overlooked the effects of mixing races, when the illustrations drawn from the crossing of animals speak so plainly—man physically is, but an animal at last, with the same physiological laws which govern others.

This adulteration of blood is the reason why Egypt and th Barbary States never can again rise, until the present races are exterminated, and the Caucasian substituted

Wherever in the history of the world the inferior races have conquered and mixed in with the Caucasian, the latter have sunk into barbarism

Greece and Rome have been conquered and crushed to the earth by oppression, but the blood of Greeks and Romans is still comparatively pure, and the genius of those nations still lives

Every now and then some one rises up, breaks through all tramels and shows that the Caucasian head is still there They have not the physical force to break the fetters which bind them, but they still have their Poets, Painters, Sculptors and Philosophers.

We have no evidence that civilization has ever eminated

from Africa beyond Egypt, and we know that all modern at
tempts to carry civilization into it have failed.

When I was in Paris I attended the Hospitals every day
in company with about a dozen young Egyptians, who were
sent over by Mehamet Ali—nothing could be more evident
than their mixed blood—some looked like mulattoes, others
like the cross of Indian and white races. When I looked upon them and saw the material with which Mehamet Ali had to
work, I was convinced that Egypt's sun of glory was set,
never again to rise

ANALOGY.—When we cast our eyes over the whole range
of natural history, we find a surprising simplicity and uniformity in the laws of nature—a wonderful adaptation of things to
the circumstances in which they are placed. This uniformity
of laws often assists us immensely when we are wanting in
facts in one branch—analogies drawn from others shed impor
tant light

In illustration of the natural history of man for instance, analogies have been drawn from the whole animal and vegitable
kingdoms, many of these analogies are curious and interesting, and they are so numerous and varied as to afford strong
arguments, both for and against the unity of the human race

Both animal and vegitable kingdoms are divided and subdi-
vided into genera, species and varieties

As we shall have frequent use for the term species, it will
be well to define it before we proceed farther

We mean then by the term Species, a race of Animals or
Plants, marked by peculiarities of structure, which have always been constant and undeviating—two races are considered specifically different, if they are distinguished from each
other by some peculiarities which one cannot be supposed
to have acquired, or the other lost, through any known opera-
tion of physical causes

The Horse and Ass, for example, are the same genus, but
different species, because no physical causes could have produced such dissimilarity.

Genus, is a more comprehensive term, it includes all the
species of a class, for example, the Ourang Outang, Apes
Baboons, &c, are all of one genus though different species

My belief too, is, that there is a Genus *Homo*, with its species and varieties

It would be almost an anomaly in nature if man should be
restricted to one species

I will cite a few examples from the animal and vegitable
kingdoms for illustration

Naturalists have described 30 different species of Ape, several of the Baboon, and a number of the Monkey .This group is the nearest link to man, and when compared they do not differ more than the Caucasian, the Mongol, the Malay, the Indian and the Negro

Of the Genus *Equus*, there are 5 species, the Horse, the Ass, the Wild Mule, the Quagga and the Zebra. Of the Cat kind no less than 28

I might thus go on through the whole animal kingdom

Near the Cape of Good Hope there are 300 species of insects which are found now here else.

The same law is seen in the vegetable kingdom—look at the species of Oak, Hickory and other trees—look at our fruits, flowers, &c

The whole range of natural history proves another law, viz. that particular species of both plants and animals, are suited to certain climates and soils and no other

Islands newly emerged from the ocean, without a sprig of vegetation, soon become covered with plants, different from plants in any other part of the world, but showing a family likeness to those of the nearest mainland

Terra Australis, which is very remotely situated, has a stock of plants and animals altogether peculiar. It contains entire genera of Animals, which have not been discovered elsewhere—animals too, which are very curious in their anatomical and physiological characters—the different species of the Kangaroo, and many others

The Elephant, Rhinoceros, Hippopotamus, Giraffe, Camel, Horse—most of the Ox kind belong to the old continent exclusively Lions, Tigers, Hyenas, &c , to Asia and Africa, the Quagga and Zebra to Southern Africa

None of the above animals were found in America when discovered

Of the 28 species belonging to the Cat kind, it is very remarkable that not one is common to the Old and New World

The Opossum, the Sloths, a new tribe of Monkeys, and many other animals and plants, are peculiar to America, as well as an immense number of organic remains

To use the language of Pritchard, (the great orthodox defender of the unity of the human race,) "These various tribes are not spread over the earth by chance, or without local relations, but the different regions of the world, may be said to have given origin to peculiar kinds, adapted respectively by their organization, to subsist under the local circumstances, among which they appear first to have been called into existence"

Now I would ask, if this be a general law, by which nature is governed throughout all creation, is it reasonable that man alone should form an exception.

None of these plants and animals can be propagated out of the climate to which they are adapted by nature—and man forms no exception to the general law. The white man can not live in tropical Africa, or the African in the frigid zone.

Wherever colonies of Europeans have been formed, in temperate countries, they have soon flourished, and the white population has multiplied so fast, as to encroach upon the native, and in many instances, entirely supersede them. But in Africa, colonies of Europeans and Asiatics have dwindled away and become extinct. The coast of Zanguebar was colonized many centuries ago by Arabians, and afterwards by Portuguese—at a still earlier period by Phœnicians. Other colonies have been formed in Mozambique, Quiola, Kongo, &c. but the climate has prevented population from flourishing and multiplying. Were it not for these facts we should certainly see white colonies there like every where else, where fortune is to be gained.

On the other hand, the proofs are quite as positive to show that the negro is equally unsuited to a cold climate.

Though a constant influx of negro slaves takes place from Soudan into Turkey, it is without effect or impression.

Herodotus tells us that there was once a colony of Black woolly headed Africans at Colchis but they are extinct.

No black race in short has been, or can be established at any great distance from the equator.

Look at the bills of mortality in our northern cities, and you will see the proportion of deaths amongst the blacks, increasing as you go north until you get to Boston, where the proportion is three to one compared to the whites.

This has been attributed to their habits and condition, but if I had time I could prove positively, that climate there has its influence.

I have in another place mentioned the fact, that a cold climate so freezes their brains as to make them insane or idiotical.

Pritchard, the great orthodox naturalist of England, denies that all the animals now on the earth could have descended from Noah's Ark. He says it is irreconcilable with Zoological researches, and in this opinion every naturalist must concur.

He says further, "that it is no where asserted in the Mosaic history, and who can prove that the various nations of animals, which have the centre of their abode, and seem to have had the origin of their existence in distant regions, as Terra Australis, or South America, were not created since that Deluge, which the human race and the species of animals which were their companions survived? This indeed seems to be the conclusion, which facts every day discovered, dispose us more and more to adopt."

"It is known that the fossile remains of Animals, which have been discovered in various parts of the earth, and which appear to be relics of the Anti-Deluvian world, chiefly belonged to species, different from those which now exist, these species were probably exterminated in that great catastrophe."

"Man escaped with the stock of animals peculiar to the region in which he lived After the deluge, when new regions emerged from the ocean, it is probable they were supplied with plants and animals suited to the soil and climate of each district."

Why I would again ask, should man be made an exception to this general law?

Pritchard goes on to say, "that it is not to be presumed, that these sacred books contain a narrative of all, that it has pleased providence to effect in the physical creation, but only his dispensations to mankind, and the facts with which man is concerned—and it was of no importance for man to be informed at what era New Holland began to contain Kangaroos, or the woods of Paraguay, Ant eaters and Armadillos."

It seems, says he, "to be fully proved, by geological researches, that repeated creations have taken place, and that the organized tribes in existence have more than once perished, to make room for a new order of beings It seems probable, and in some instances evident, that these epochs or revolutions in nature, have been accompanied, or preceded by inundations and other catastrophes Such events may have contributed to prepare the earth for supporting new tribes of organized creatures After each of these changes in its physical condition, it has given birth to races different from those which before existed, and adapted to the circumstances of its new state We may therefore conclude, that after, the last deluge, a similar renewal of the animal and vegitable kingdoms ensued"

"That this was really the fact, may be collected from an examination of the organic remains of the anti-deluvian world"

All naturalists admit the following facts "The remains of animals found in the oldest strata, or those deposited in the earliest period are known to display a very simple structure, and are very remote from the present forms At successive periods, the nature of animals became more complete, or rather more complicate, and more approaching those at present in existence Many of the species which existed before the flood, are now extinct, and new ones have risen up—nearly all the carnivora for instance, are post deluvian "

Now it will be seen by these extracts, that Mr. P. has been compelled to distort the Mosaic account to reconcile it with positive, indisputable, scientific facts He has abandoned the whole Mosaic account of the creation of the Heavens, the earth, and every thing upon it, but man

And why should man alone be retained? Simply, because the facts have been wanting to establish distinct species Mr Pritchard has argued the question fairly—he has yielded every point in science which has been proven, and no doubt will give up the unity of the human race when sufficient facts can be adduced. He has at least, by his admissions, thrown the question fairly open for discussion

But we will pass on to some analogies which are more familiar.

Some very curious and striking analogies have been brought forward from the animal kingdom to prove, that physical causes, have produced changes in color, hair, form and instincts, quite as great as those which are seen in the human race—the varieties in Rabbits, Cats, Dogs, Oxen, Foxes, Fowls &c &c have been cited

All the swine in Piedmont, are black, in Normandy white, in Bavaria brown The Oxen in Hungary are gray, in Franconia red Horses and dogs in Corsica are spotted the Turkies of Normandy are black, those of Hanover white, &c — The dray horse of London and the Shetland Poney, are the same species The Wild Boar and Berkshire, the large cock and the Bantom, the long legged Ox of the Cape of Good Hope, and the Durham, &c

One of the most striking instances is the variety of Dogs, which are *supposed* to be of but one species The New Foundland, the Bull, the Grey Hound, the Pointer, the Terrier, Poodle, &c, certainly differ in their heads, form, size, color, hair, instincts, &c, as much as the different varieties of men—a more striking illustration of the effects of physical causes, could not be given

Now all these changes we freely admit, but does this prove that physical causes have the same power to change man? If climate, food and other physical causes can thus change man, why, I would ask, have they not done it? And why cannot the written history of the world for two thousand years adduce instances?

The human race have been living in the same places where these mighty changes have been effected in animals, and still man is comparatively unchanged. Why in these countries are men so much alike and animals so different? The answer is that human constitutions are less mutable, and men have the power and means of protecting themselves by houses, clothing, fires, &c, against the action of such causes

Why should all the asserted changes in the human race have taken place in ages beyond the reach of history Will any one pretend that human nature is not the same now that it was 5,000 years ago? And that the same physical causes have not been at work?

Tradition speaks of migrations, floods, wars and great convulsions in nature—it tells of fiery dragons, hydras, giants and other monsters, but no where are we told that the Ethiopian has changed his skin—even poetry and fable are silent on this point

LECTURE II

PHYSICAL DIFFERENCES.—The Anatomical and Physiological differences, between the Caucasian, the Malay, Mongol, Indian and Negro races, have elicited a great deal of scientific research, and I might very well write an octavo on these points alone. Time, however, compels me to restrict my lecture to a parallel between the Caucasian and Negro races. I wish it further to be understood, that my parallel will be limited to the race of Negroes which we see in this country, and which I shall presently describe. There are many other tribes in Africa, which differ widely in color, physical and intellectual characters.

When the Caucasian and Negro are compared, one of the most striking and important points of difference is seen in the conformation of the head.

The head of the Negro is smaller by a full tenth—the forehead is narrower and more receding, in consequence of which the anterior or intellectual portion of the brain is defective.— The upper jaw is broader and more projecting—the under jaw inclines out, and is deficient in chin; the lips are larger and correspond with the bony structure; the teeth point obliquely forward and resemble in shape those of Carnivorous animals; the bones of the head are thicker, more dense and heavy, and the same fact exists with regard to the other bones of the skeleton.

Dr. Gall, in his laborious researches, has established the important fact, which is now conceded, that there is in the animal kingdom, a regular gradation in the form of the brain, from the Caucasian down to the lowest order of animals, and that the intellectual faculties and instincts are commensurate with the size and form. *

In animals where the senses and sensual faculties predomi-

Note.—I beg leave here once for all to state that I have never studied and do not advocate the details of Phrenology, but no one doubts that the brain is the organ of intellect and instinct, and that the *general* facts of Phrenology are true.

nate, the nerves coming off from the brain are large, and we find the nerves of the Negro larger than those of the Caucasian.

In other portions of the skeleton, differences not less marked, are presented. The arm of the African is much longer than in the Caucasian—a Negro of 5 feet 6 has an arm as long as a white man of 6 feet. The arm from the elbow to the hand is much longer in proportion, than in the white man—his hand is longer, more bony and tendinous—the nails more projecting and stronger.

The chest of the negro is more compressed laterally, and deeper through from before backwards—the bones of the pelvis in the male are more slender and narrow, the muscles on the sides of the pelvis are less full, but more full posteriorly.

In the two races the lower limbs are in their relative proportion reversed—in their *entire* measurement, the legs of the African are shorter, but the thigh longer and flatter—the bones at the knee joint instead of being straight, are joined at an obtuse angle, pointing forward. The shape of the shin bone, calf, foot and heel, are familiar to you all *

Now it will be seen from this hasty sketch, how many points of resemblance Anatomists have established between the Negro and Ape. It is seen in the head and face, the arms and hands, the compressed chest, the bones and muscles of the pelvis, the flat long thighs, the forward bend of the knee, in the leg, foot and toes. In short, place beside each other average specimens of the Caucasian, Negro and Ourang Outang and you will perceive a regular and striking gradation—substitute for the Negro a Bushman or Hottentot from the Cape of Good Hope and the contrast is still stronger.

"In the Bushman (says Lichtenstein) all the deformities of the race are seen in an exaggerated degree they are extremely diminutive—4 feet 6 inches high. Their flat nose, high cheek bones, prominent chin, and concave visage give them much of the Apish character which is increased by their keen, vivid

Note.—It has been asserted that each race shows instances of the physical characters which belong to the others. I admit that the best specimens of Negroes are very like the inferior of the Caucasian, but when you compare extremes the argument fails—actual measurements show that Negroes never have heads so large and well formed as those of Cuvier and Dupuytren and who ever saw a white man resemble the exaggerated specimens of Negroes—the gradation seen in the old continent may depend upon the intermixture of races originally widely different but admitting the argument in its full force it amounts to nothing. The Wolf Dog and Hyena or Tiger and Panther which are distinct species present physical difference previous to dissect.

eye, always on the alert—they spring from rock to rock with the activity of Antelopes—sleep in nests which they form in bushes, just like bird's nests, but seldom pass two nights in the same place. They live by depredation, or by catching wild animals, such as serpents, lizards, ants, grass hoppers, &c.—They too, have humps on their backs like Dromedaries."

The difference to an Anatomist, between the Bushman or Negro and the Caucasian, is greater than the difference in the skeletons of the Wolf, Dog and Hyena, which are allowed to be distinct species, or the Tiger and Panther.

Now can all these deep, radical and enduring differences be produced by climate and other causes assigned? It is incumbent on those who contend for such an opinion, to show that such changes either *have* taken place, or that similar changes in the *human race are now in progress.*

It is now 1,700 years since the Jews were banished from their native country, and soon after this event a colony of them settled on the coast of Malabar, amongst a people whose color was black, they were visited a few years ago by Dr Claudius Buchanan, who states in his travels, that in complexion form and features, they still preserve the characteristics of the Jews of Europe—the natives too are still unchanged*

More than 1000 years ago, a colony of Persians were driven into India by religious persecution—they settled amongst a people of black complexion, like the Jews, they have been prevented by religious tenets, from intermarrying with the natives. Their descendants in that burning climate, we are informed by Col Wilks, who is familiar with this people, are a fine race of men, perfectly Caucasian in complexion, form and feature—altogether unlike those around them.

The same facts are observed in the Portuguese colonies in Mozambique and Zanguebar, on the Eastern Coast of Tropical Africa.

The Spanish settlements in Tropical America and the English settlements in the West Indies, present the same facts—great numbers have died from the effect of climate—the complexion has lost its rudiness, and their skins have become swarthy and bilious—their frames have become attenuated be-

*Note—It appears by their records, which were considered by Dr Buchanan to be *authentic* that they emigrated to India soon after the destruction of the Temple of Jerusalem by Titus, and that they afterwards obtained grants of territory and privileges, of which they have documents bearing date in the year A M 4250 or A D 490. The black Jews he states are a mixed race, descended in great part from the natives of the country, whom they resemble in physical character.—*Christian Researches in Asia.*

cause nature never intended them for this climate, but their features are still the same. Their children are born fair, and if carried to a temperate climate, would remain so. Every thing goes to prove that there is a limit to the effect of climate. The Caucasian though effected to a certain extent by climate, cannot be transformed into a negro, or a negro into an Ourang Outang.

The Moors have inhabited some parts of Tropical Africa from time immemorial, yet neither in complexion, feature, form, hair, or in any thing else, have they made any approximation towards the Negro.

The Chinese, the Hindoos, the Jews, the Gipsies and numerous other tribes, afford strong illustrations, but I have no time to dwell upon them.

It is about two centuries since the Africans were introduced into this country, the 8th or 9th generation is now amongst us, and the race is unchanged. The Negroes have been improved by comforts and good feeding which they have been unaccustomed to; but they are Negroes still.

A large portion of Oceanica, where the climate is temperate and pleasant, is inhabited by Negroes, who no doubt, have dwelt there for ages.

New South Wales extends beyond the 39th degree of south latitude, and many parts of it have a remarkably healthy and delightful climate, yet the following is the description given by Malt-Brun of its natives.

"New South Wales seems to offer three native varieties of inhabitants, all belonging to the race of Oceanean negroes. In the neighborhood of Glass House Bay, the savages have large heads, which in shape resemble those of the Ourang Outang, their very limited intellects, hairy bodies, and habitual agility in climbing trees, seem to bring them very near to the Ape character."

What too are the facts with regard to the aborigines of America? I will here give some facts from Dr. Morton's Crania Americana.

Although, says he, the Americans possess a pervading and characteristic complexion, there are occasional and very remarkable deviations, including all the tints from a decided white to an unequivocally black skin. He shows also, by numerous authorities, that climate exerts a *subordinate* agency in producing these diversified hues. The tribes which wander along the burning plains of the equinoctial region, have no darker skins than the mountaineers of the temperate zone — Again, the Puelches and other inhabitants of the Megallanic region, beyond the 55th degree of South Latitude are also solutely darker than the Abipones, Macobios and Tobas, who are many degrees nearer the Equator While the Botocudys are of a clear brown color, and sometimes nearly white at no great distance from the Tropic, and moreover, while the Guyacas, under the line are characterised by a fair complexion, the Charruas, who are almost black, inhabit the 50th degree of South Latitude, and the yet blacker Californians are 25 degrees north of the Equator. *After all*, he adds, these differences in complexion are *extremely partial*, forming mere *exceptions* to the primitive and national tint, that characterises these people from Cape Horn to the Canadas.

The cause of the anomalies is not readily explained; that it is not climate, is sufficiently obvious, and whether it arises from partial immigrations from other countries, remains yet to be decided."

With respect to the Polynesian tribes it has been remarked by Marsden and Crawford, that the heat of the climate seems to have no connection with the darkness of the complexion, the fairest natives in most instances, are those situated nearest the Equator

If we inquire into the history of the Papua and Australian tribes with relation to this point, we shall find that the complexion does not become regularly lighter, as we recede from the intertropical clime—for the people of Van Dieman's Land, who are the most distant from the equator are black

The Tartars are brown and the Europeans white in the same latitude.

It is well known to the naturalist that the skins of the white and black races differ widely in their anatomical and physiological characters, but details on this point would here be out of place The skin in all the races is composed of several lamina—the outer is called the cuticle, and is thin and transparent—the second is a vascular net work, called the Rete Mucosum, and it is on this that the color of the skin depends—it secretes a black pigment or paint which gives the black skin to the negro, and it will from this be seen that the blackness *cannot* be caused by the rays of the sun producing a change in its color. In a sailor or out door laborer, who is exposed to the sun the skin is, as we express it, tanned or burnt—becomes dark, but there is none of this pigment secreted and the change in the father is not transmitted to the child

Another striking fact is seen in negro children—when born they are almost as fair as a white child, but in a very short time and without any exposure to the sun, this black pigment is secreted, and the skin becomes black—here is a function different from any in the whites.

The skin of the African too, is known to generate less heat, and he therefore stands a hot climate better, and a cold worse than the white man

We are all familiar also, with the *bouquet odour* of a negro's skin, which cannot be accounted for by accidental causes.

In this discussion great weight has been given to the admitted fact, that the color of the skin in the old world, is generally found to accord with climate. The white man is found in the cold and temperate regions, the black in the torrid zone, and the intermediate complexions between the two.

There are however, as we have seen, so many exceptions to the rule as to destroy it

Moreover, if different pairs of the human race, of different complexions and physical conformations, were placed by the creator in the positions best suited to their organization, they would naturally multiply and spread—after a e the different races would come in contact, mingle together and form intermediate varieties. In fact this is a picture of what is now going on all over the world I have been often struck by the resemblance of the colored creoles in New Orleans, to the Mongol race—many of them have the high cheek bones, oblique eyes and other characteristics.

If the position I take be true, that the human race is descended from *several* or *many* original pairs, it is reasonable to suppose that there is not at present a single unmixed race on the face of the earth.*

Look at the population of the United States¹ From how many nations have we received crosses? Read the early history of Great Britain, France, Germany, Egypt, in short the whole world as far as we have records—who now can tell what blood predominates in each nation?

Much stress has been laid upon the variety of complexions, hair and conformation, seen in what is *supposed to be* the same race Take England for example, where you find people of very different features and forms—the complexions vary from fair to tawney, and the hair from blond to black.

These facts have been cited to show that varieties spring

* Note —It has been *supposed* that the varieties of the human race, were produced at the Tower of Babel, when the confusion of tongues occurred but so remarkable an occurrence would have been mentioned We might just as well *suppose* that some were changed into Monkeys, while others were changed into negroes In arguing a question of this kind we want *facts*

up in the same race, which if separated and allowed to multiply alone, would make permanent varieties as distinct as the Caucasian, Mongol and Negro. But I would ask, how much of this may not be attributable to mingling of races originally different?

Every man conversant with the breeding of Horses, Cattle, Dogs and sheep, is aware of the effect of the slightest taint of impure blood—there are no data by which we can determine the length of time which it will endure. An English turfman will not own a horse whose pedigree cannot be traced back to the remotest records of pure blood, and what is remarkable, no horse has ever been the progenitor of successful runners, who has been *known to have one drop* of impure blood in his veins. The celebrated race horse Plenipo, is a fac simile of one of his ancestors 8 generations back, and unlike the intermediate links. A strong likeness is sometimes remarked in race horses, to the Godolphin Arabian, who was brought to England, over a hundred years ago. Look at the family portraits of the Bourbon family, and many others in Europe—though they have been intermarrying with other families for generations, the likeness is still preserved.

A very curious fact may be cited to prove how strong an impression is made upon the offspring, by a cause too slight to be conceived of. It is known to be a fact that a mare has produced a colt from a Quagga, and her next colt from a horse has been striped like a Quagga, though having no relationship whatever that we can imagine.

Man and animals are doubtless governed by the same general physiological laws, and no one can calculate the results which may arise from crossing races. My belief is, that the human race are descended from original stocks, which were essentially different—that these original stocks were placed by an Allwise Creator in the climate and situation best suited to their organization.

The black man was placed in Tropical Africa, because he was suited to this climate and no other. The white man was placed in Europe and Asia, for the same reason. I have elsewhere given facts to prove this. The statistics of our northern cities show that the proportion of deaths amongst the blacks, compared to the whites, is nearly three to one. Facts of a different nature and not less astounding, have recently been published in the Southern Literary Messenger, taken from authentic statistics.

Among the slave population of Louisiana, the insane and idiots number 1 in 4,310, in South Carolina 1 in 2,477, in Va gina 1 in 1,299; but what a different picture is presented at the North—in Massachusetts there is in that class of population, 1 insane or idiot, in 43, and in Maine, 1 in 14!!!!!

Now much of this is attributable to climate, but not all is I shall show hereafter. In the Northern cities there is a large proportion of Mulattoes, who I regard and shall attempt to prove, are *Hybrids.* These Hybrids we *know* to be shorter lived than the whites or blacks, and probably more prone to insanity—but the *facts* stand, and construe them as you please, they go strongly to prove the existence of distinct species in the human race.

QUESTION OF HYBRIDS.—A *hybrid* off-spring is the strongest and most unequivocal proof of the distinctness of species. The mule for instance is the hybrid offspring of the horse and ass, its inability to produce offspring, and other peculiarities, leave no doubt that the parent stocks are distinct species.

In an article which I published in the July number of the American Medical Journal, I brought forward a number of facts to prove that the *Mulatto was a hybrid,* and as a necessary inference, that the white and negro races were now, if not always, distinct species. As these facts are very intimately connected with the subject of the present lecture, I will here recapitulate them with some additions, and will first give an extract from a very sensible article published in the spring of '43, in the Boston Medical and Surgical Journal, under signature of "philanthropist."

The writer says From authentic statistics and extensive corroborating information obtained from sources to me of *unquestionable authority,* together with my own observations, I am led to believe that the following statements are substantially correct:

1st. That the longevity of the Africa s is greater than that of the inhabitants of any other part of the Globe.

2d. That *Mulattoes,* (i e) those born of parents one being African and the other white or Caucasian, are the *shortest lived of any class of the human race.*

3d. That the Mulattoes are not more liable to die under the age of 25, than the whites or blacks, *but from 25 to 40 their deaths are as 10 to 1, of either the whites or blacks between those ages—from 40 to 55 the deaths are 50 to 1, and from 55 to 70, 100 to 1.*

4th. That the mortality of the free people of color is more than 100 per cent greater than that of slaves.

5th That those of unmixed extraction in the free states, are not more liable to sickness, or premature death, than the whites of their rank and condition in society, but that the striking mortality, so manifest amongst the free people of color, is in every community and section of the country, *invariably confined to the Mulattoes*

"It was remarked by a gentleman from the south, eminent for his intellectual attainments, and distinguished for his correct observation, and who has lived many years in the Southern States, that he did not believe that he had ever seen a mulatto of 70 years of age."

From a correspondence published in the Boston statesman, in April list, are taken the following statistics.

In a colored population of 2,631,518 including free blacks, there are 1,980 over 100 years of age, whereas there are but 647 whites over 100, in a population of 11,681,000

Dr. Niles in a pamphlet published in 1827, gave a comparative statement of mortality in the cities of Philadelphia, New York and Baltimore, deduced from official reports of the Boards of Health of the respective cities, from which it appears that in the years 1823, 4, 5 and 6, the deaths were as follows

	New York	Philadelphia	Baltimore
Whites	1 in 46	1 in 3182	1 in 11,29
Free blacks	1 in 48	1 in 19,91	1 in 52
Slaves,			1 in 70

In Boston the amount of mortality among the colored population is about 1 in 45, and there are fewer pure blacks in this city than any other. The same comparative mortality between Mulattoes and blacks exists at the West In dies and Guaiana, where unfavorable social causes do not operate against the Mulattoes, as in the United States."

Fifteen years professional intercourse and observation have led me to conclusions which correspond very closely with those of Philanthropist—I would add

1st That the mulattoes are intermediate in intelligence between the blacks and whites

2d. That they are less capable of undergoing fatigue and hardships, than the blacks or whites

3d That the mulatto women are particularly delicate, and subject to a variety of chronic diseases

4th That the women are bad breeders and bad nurses—many do not conceive—most are subject to abortions, and a large portion of the children die young in the southern States

5th That the two sexes when they intermarry, are less prolific than when crossed on one of the parent stocks

6th That Negroes and mulattoes are exempt in a surprising degree from yellow fever

The subject of hybrids, is a very curious one, on which much might be said, but we have space only for a few general remarks

There are a great variety of hybrids, running through the whole chain of animated nature, in both animal and vegetable kingdoms Some hybrids do not breed—as the Mule for example There are rare instances of them having propagated when crossed back, on one of the parent stocks There are other hybrids, which do propagate perfectly—as the offspring of the Goat and Ewe—the Goldfinch and Canary bird—the Cygnoides (Chinese Goose) and the common Goose, &c. &c

Those hybrids, (which do breed) when bred together, have a tendency to run out, and change back to one of the parent stocks—the hybrid geese for instance, if kept alone, degenerate into common geese in a very few generations This has been remarked too, in the mulattoes of the West Indies and there are now families in Mobile from the same parents, some of whom are nearly black, and others nearly white, where there is every reason to believe that the mothers have been faithful to their husbands

Another general law laid down by naturalists, is, that the hybrid derives its size and internal structure principally from the mother, a striking example of which is given in the mule

The mule or offspring of the Mare and Ass, is a large and powerful animal, having the internal organization of the mother The Bardeau, or hinny, on the contrary, (the offspring of the Horse and Jenny) is a small and comparatively worthless animal.

Buffon and other Naturalists assert also, that in hybrids the head resembles the father. A familiar illustration may be again seen in the Mule. The offspring of the Ass and Mare, has the long ears, large coarse head, expression and other peculiarities of his dignified progenitor. In the Bardeau, on the contrary the head of the horse is preserved—it is long and lean, with short ears. This law has an important bearing on the subject now before us.

It is well settled by naturalists, that the brain of the Negro, when compared with the Caucasian, is smaller by a tenth, and is particularly defective in the anterior or intellectual lobes, and that the intellect is wanting in the same proportion. In the white race the fact is notorious, that the child derives its intellect much more from the mother than the father—it is an old remark that a stupid mother never produces an intelligent family of children. Look the world over and ask who are the mothers of the eminent men, and it will be found that there are few exceptions to the rule that the mothers are above, and most of them far above mediocrity.

But this important law of nature is reversed when the white man is crossed upon the Negress or Indian woman—the law of hybrids is shown at once—in the offspring the brain is enlarged, the facial angle increased, and the intellect improved in a marked degree. Every one at the south is familiar with the fact that the mulattoes have more intelligence than negroes, make bad slaves, and are always leaders in insurrections.

Estwick and Long, the historians of Jamaica, both state unhesitatingly, that the male and female mulatto do not produce together so many children, as when they are united respectively to Negresses and Europeans. I am credibly informed that these facts are very strikingly verified in New Orleans, where there is a mixture of the races to great extent. I am told that it is not uncommon to see a family run out so completely, as to leave estates without heirs to claim them.

I have called attention in another part of my lecture to some interesting statistics to show the effect of cold climate and social condition combined in producing idiocy and insanity in the free blacks of the northern States. I have no facts yet to ground an opinion upon, but I have little doubt that it will be found that these effects, like disease and early deaths, are confined mostly to the mulattoes. I have shown that in Maine, 1 in 14, and in Massachusetts 1 in 43, are lunatics or idiots, of the colored population.

As different hybrids are acknowledged to be governed by different laws, is it not reasonable to believe that the human hybrid may also have its peculiar laws?—may not one of these laws be (which is a reasonable inference from foregoing data) that the mulatto is a degenerate, unnatural offspring, doomed by nature to work out its own destruction. The statistics of Philanthropist prove that the mulattoes are shorter lived, and it is an every day remark at the South, that they are more liable to be diseased and are less capable of endurance than either whites or blacks of the same rank and condition.

What then could we expect in breeding from a faulty stock, a stock which has been produced by a violation of nature's laws, but that they should become more and more degenerate in each succeeding generation? We know that the parent will transmit to the child, not only his external form, character, expression, temperament, &c., but diseases, through many generations, as insanity, gout, scrofula, consumption, &c. Why then may not that defect in internal organization which leads to ultimate destruction exist in the mulatto? I believe that if a hundred white men and one hundred black women were put together on an Island, and cut off from all intercourse with the rest of the world, they would in time become extinct.

It has been asserted by writers that when the grade of Quinteroon is arrived at, all trace of black blood is lost and they cannot be distinguished from the whites. Now if this be true, most of the mulattoes must cease to be prolific, before this point of mixture is arrived at—for though I have passed most of my life in places where the two races have been mingling for 8 or 9 generations, I have rarely, if ever met an individual tainted with negro blood, in whom I could not detect it without difficulty.—these higher grades should be extremely common, if the chain was not broken by death and sterility—how else can the fact be accounted for?

These &c. distinguished J. have in a disc. states that the connections between the Europeans and women of New Holland are rarely prolific.

The different races in America have been mixing together from time immemorial, and we have no yet no facts from which to form an opinion on the question, whether there are affinities between certain races or species which make them intermix better than others, or to what extent the law of hybrids prevail? In a word applies to other parts of the world as well as this.

MORAL AND INTELLECTUAL.—One cannot but myself references

have been shown to be, between the races of men, the intellectual and moral disparity is perhaps still greater

I have already alluded to the fact that the brain is known to be the organ on which the mind of man and the instinct of animals depend, and that the perfection of those faculties is commensurate with the perfect organization of this organ.— There is a marked difference between the heads of the Caucasian and the Negro, and there is a corresponding difference no less marked in their intellectual and moral qualities

The brain of the Negro, as I have stated is, according to positive measurements, smaller than the Caucasian by a full tenth, and this deficiency exists particularly in the anterior portion of the brain, which is known to be the seat of the higher faculties History and observation both teach that in accordance with this defective organization the Mongol, the Malay, the Indian and Negro, are now and have been in all ages and all places, inferior to the Caucasian

Look at the world as it now stands and say where is civilization to be found except amongst the various branches of the Caucasian race?

Take Europe and start in the freezing climate of Russia, and come down to the straights of Gibralter, and you find not a solitary exception, not one that excites a doubt

Take Asia in the same way, and the only approximation to civilization, is found in the mass, of persons of the Mongol tribes Take China which is the nearest approximation—she has for centuries had stability in her government, and many of the arts have been carried to a high state of perfection, but take her religion, her laws, her government her literature, and how does the comparison stand? The most you can say is, that the Chinese are an intermediate link between the Negro and Caucasian

Take Africa next and the picture presented is only deplorable—with the exception of Egypt and the Barbary States, which were in their palmy day occupied by Caucasian colonies, and now by their mixed descendants and where I repeat, except here, will you find from the Mediterranean to the Cape of Good Hope, a single record or a single monument to show that civilization has ever existed? Where are the ruins of her Memphis, her Thebes, her Rome, her Athens or her Carthage Their intellects are now as they always have been, as dark as their skins

Carthage, once the proud rival of Rome, has often been cited as an instance of what a negro race is capable but we now know that Carthage, like Egypt was a Caucasian colony from Asia, and has been constantly going downwards since her people have been conquered and adulterated in blood by African hordes

Cyprian, Augustine, Hannibal, Æsop, Euclid and others, have been brought up as evidences of African intellects, but all history would prove that they were as different from the genuine Negro, as they were from the American Indian

Let us next look nearer home—America when discovered by Columbus, was populated by millions of Aborigines from one extreme to the other—taking in the whole range of latitude Much has been written about the ruined cities of Central America, and endless speculations have been indulged in respecting their antiquity, the people who built them, their degree of civilization, &c

From the accumulated information of Spanish historians, and from the laborious researches of Stephens, we are forced to believe that these cities were built by the same people who inhabited these countries when they were conquered by Cortez and the Pizarros. And what was their condition then?—they lived in the cities which they had built and which are now in ruins What was the condition amongst them of the arts, sciences, and literature? What their religion, government and laws? Every thing proves that they were miserable imbeciles, very far below the Chinese of the present day in every particular

There is nothing in the whole history of romance, so rich in interesting incident as the conquest of these countries —Cortez landed in Mexico with only 500 men, and determined to conquer or die, he burned his own ships to cut off all hope of retreat, he then started off for the city of Mexico, and after fighting his way with his little band, through millions of this miserable race, he entered Mexico, seized Montezuma in his palace and threw him into chains The conquest of Peru is still more interesting if possible, but this is not the place to dwell on such topics I merely allude to it to show what the population were, and to show that 500 Caucasian arms and heads were worth more than millions of these miserable creatures

Many of the remains of this people are stupendous and show considerable Architectural skill, but my conviction is that too much importance has been attached to Architectural remains The talent of constructiveness may be developed in a very high degree, but without the higher faculties of comparison and causality necessarily being in proportion The beaver, many birds, and insects show this talent in a surprising degree —

Read the Natural history of the Honey Bee, and you will see things almost as remarkable as any thing we have spoken of in Central America—Chiapas, Yucatan, Mexico, &c

The Queen Bee when she passes through her dominion is bowed to by her subjects with all the respect and submission shown to an Eastern Princess If the Queen Bee dies, the news is spread throughout the hive—all is consternation and commotion until another is elected and quietly seated on the throne—if there is no suitable candidate, an egg is chosen and placed in an enlarged cell, and as soon as the infant Queen is hatched, she is fed on a rich and peculiar kind of food A Queen is thus reared who is of larger size, and of entirely different form and appearance from the populace. The drones too, and the laboring class have their appropriate duties assigned them, which they perform with a regularity and exactness unknown in the human race The *dwellings* of the Bee are constructed on a regular plan and on perfect *mathematical principles.* If a part of the honey-comb is cracked by the interference of man, the laborers are called up and set to work to repair the injury—a prop is constructed with all the science of a Christopher Wren, or Michael Angelo, in short, every thing in the history of the Bee shows a reasoning power little short of that of a Mexican.

But what does the history of the Caucasian show in all climes and in all times—strike off the fetters of bad government, and he takes up the march of civilization and presses onward—the principle of action within him is like the life in the acorn—take an acorn which has laid in a box for a thousand years and plant it in a congenial soil, it sprouts at once and grows into the majestic oak.

History cannot designate the time when the Caucasian was a savage—Caucasian races have often been plunged by circumstances into barbarism, but never as far as we know, into savageism Cannibalism appears to belong exclusively to the African and Oceanic Negroes—the Bushman, the Hottentots, and perhaps the Caribs but history does not tell us when and where the Caucasian has gorged his appetite on human flesh and blood

We can carry back the history of the Negro (though imperfectly) for 4,000 years we know that he had all the physical characteristics then which he has now, and we have good grounds for believing that he was morally and intellectually the same then as now One generation does not take up civilization where the last left it and carry it on as does the Caucasian—there it stands immovable they go as far as instinct extends and no farther. Where, or when I would ask, has a negro left his impress upon the age in which he lived? Can any reasoning mind believe that the Negro and Indian have always been the victim of circumstances? No, nature has endowed them with an inferior organization, and all the powers of earth cannot elevate them above their destiny.

Imperfect as the civilization of St. Domingo now is, if you were to abstract the white blood which exists amongst them they would sink at once into savagism.

The Indian is by nature a savage, and a beast of the forest like the Buffalo—can exist in no other state, and is exterminated by the approach of civilization. You cannot make a slave of him like a negro, his spirit is broken and he dies like a wild animal in a cage.

In spite of all that has been said to the contrary, facts prove that every attempt to educate and civilize the Indian, but makes him more worthless and corrupt—they learn readily all the vices of the white man but never his virtues. Read the history of the Indians in New York and New England—numerous and well directed efforts were made to better their condition—where are they now—what has philanthropy done—let the graves of the Indian speak. Not one has been enough civilized to write the history of his unfortunate race.

Now let us see what truth there is in the boasted civilization of the Cherokee and Chickasaw, their destiny too is fulfilled, and their days numbered. It will be seen that whatever improvement exists in their condition is attributable to a mixture of races. Their Chiefs and Rulers are whites and mixed bloods, and the full blood Indian is now what he always has and always will be.

I will here give an extract from a very able report of Congress by the committee on Indian affairs. "The number of those who control the government of the Cherokees, are understood not to exceed 25 or 30 persons. These together with their families, and immediate dependants and connexions, may be said to constitute the whole commonwealth, so far as any real advantage may be said to attend their new system of government. Besides this class also, which embraces all the large fortune holders, there are about 200 families constituting the middle class. This class is composed of the Indians of mixed blood, and white men with Indian wives. All of them have some property and may be said to live in some degree of comfort. The committee are not aware that a single Indian of unmixed blood belongs to the two higher classes of the Cherokees. The third class of the free population is compos ed of Indians properly so denominated, who like their brethren of the red race every where else, exhibit the same characteristic traits of unconquerable indolence, improvidence and inordinate love of ardent spirits."

George Guess, the Cherokee Cadmus, has been brought forward as an instance to prove the equality of the Indian with the Caucasian intellect He saw a man reading a letter and as soon as he conceived the idea that letters could thus be made signs of ideas, he determined to make his own a written language He accordingly shut himself up in his hut for several months—invented an alphabet and put it in practice This was certainly a very remarkable effort of genius, but the father of this Cadmus, was a Scotchman,—a very important fact which has been omitted by most of those who have discoursed so pathetically about Indians

If I had time I could multiply the proofs of the moral and intellectual inferiority of the Negro and Indian when compared with the Caucasian

AFFINITY OF LANGUAGES AND RELIGIONS —Volumes have been written on the affinity of languages and religions, to prove the common origin of races, but to my mind nothing can be more fallacious—the faintest resemblances in grammatical construction, or in particular words, have been seized with avidity and confidently put forth as evidence of a common origin Is it not, however, more reasonable to believe that in ancient times (as in the present) the nations who were most civilized, stamped their characters, both in language and religion, upon the inferior tribes with whom they held communication We loose sight too much of the fact that human nature has always been the same, and are too apt to believe that the present generations are wiser than their progenitors, and that important modifications now exist in men and customs which have not existed before.

Egypt is the earliest point of civilization, and from her Greece and Rome drew their religions, and much of their languages. In their turns Greece and Rome conquered the world and spread their languages and customs wherever they went When Egypt had the power to conquer all the nations around her—to build the cities of Memphis and Thebes—to erect the Pyramids and make Astronomical calculations—when too she was sufficiently versed in maratime knowledge to carry on commerce with the East Indies, can we doubt that her religion and language were scattered over the known world? There are also strong reasons for believing that America was not unknown to the Ancient Egyptians

4

Look at the untiring labors of Christian Missionaries—they are planting our language and religion in every uncivilized nation on earth

If a great physical or moral revolution should again occur in the world like many which have occurred, it might be assumed that the Negro colonies in Liberia are descended from the English, because their language and religion are the same

This question however, is settled by the fact that there are languages in Africa which have no affinity with any other

RECAPITULATION —1 I have shown that it is proven beyond a doubt, that instead of one, there have been many creations, and that each successive creation has placed upon the earth entire new Genera, and species of Animals and plants, different from those which existed before

2. I have shown that there is good reason to believe that there have been creations in the Animal and Vegetable kingdoms since the flood of Noah

3 I have shown that these facts do not necessarily conflict with the Old or New Testament

4 I have shown by historical facts that Negroes existed 4 000 years ago with the same physical Characteristics which belong to them now

5 I have shown, that though it may exist no relationship can be traced between them and Noah's family

6 I have shown that all history proves that the Negro never has nor never can live out of a warm climate, or the white man in Tropical Africa

7 I have shown that the Caucasian and Negro differ in their Anatomical and Physiological characters, and that both written history and natural history prove that these differences could not be produced by climate and other physical causes

8 I have shown by Analogies from the Vegetable and Animal kingdoms, that there ought to be different species in the human race

9. I have shown that there now exists and has existed, as far as history speaks, a marked moral and intellectual disparity between the races, and that a high state of civilization never has existed in any other than the Caucasian race

10 I have shown that there are good grounds for believing that the varieties of men seen in any particular country, and the physical approximation seen in different tribes, originate in the mingling of different races

11 I have shown that similarity in language and religion proves nothing

12 I have shown that there are strong facts to prove that the Mulatto is a hybrid

Now if I have not fully demonstrated each and all of these positions, I think I have brought forward facts enough to prove that I have rational grounds for believing in the truth of the proposition with which I set out, viz: That there is a Genus, Man, comprising two or more species—that physical causes cannot change a white man into a negro, and that to say this change has been effected by a direct act of providence, is an assumption which cannot be proven, and is contrary to the great chain of Natures Laws.

The question will no doubt be asked *cui bono?* for what useful end has this vexed question of the Unity of Man, been torn open? In reply I would say that this is not a question for mere idle discussion, but one involving others of deep Political, Moral and Religious import.

If there be several *species* of the human race—if these species differ in the perfection of their moral and intellectual endowments—if there be a law of nature opposed to the mingling of the white and black races—I say if all these things be true, what an unexplored field is opened to the view of the Philanthropist! Is it not the *Christians duty* to inquire into this subject?

That the Negro and Indian races are susceptible of the same degree of civilization that the Caucasian is, all history would show not to be true—that the Caucasian race is deteriorated by intermixing with the inferior races is equally true.

The white and black races are now living together in the United States under circumstances which, if we may judge by the signs of the times cannot endure always and it is time for the Philanthropist to do as I have done look the question boldly in the face. What future course will be the wisest and most humane I must leave to wiser heads than mine but of this I am convinced, that nothing *wise can be done* without giving due weight to the *marked differences* which exist between the races.

Some no doubt will be disposed to censure me for the freedom with which I have handled this question and for opposing opinions which time has rendered venerable and sacred, but to me the laws of God, written in the Book of Nature are more venerable, and truth more sacred than all which emanates from erring Man.

"All Nature is but Art, unknown to thee
All chance Direction which thou canst not see
All Discord Harmony not understood
All partial Evil universal Good
And spite of Pride in erring Reason's spite
One truth is clear WHATEVER IS IS RIGHT

While my pamphlet is passing through the press the January number of the American Journal of Medical Sciences came to hand. It contains an article by Dr. Edward Jarvis on *Insanity among the colored population of the free States* in which he points out important errors in the census of the United States, which contain the statistics from which I have drawn my facts on this point. How far the Strictures of Dr Jarvis are correct I do not know, but admitting them, it would seem as if *climate* still shows its influence—but I say once more I have no cherished theory to sustain let facts be examined let us have the truth the whole truth and nothing but the truth

APPENDIX.

Company, villanous company hath been the spoil of me "

I will now add to my crime of *heresy*, by turning Judas and betraying my teachers. I should be ashamed to make such an acknowledgment, but I confess honestly that I was amazed at the objections which some have made to my lectures; for so deep have I been plunged in iniquity, that I did not know it was a sin to believe in the truths of Geology and Natural History.

It is a principle in human nature to desire companions even in misfortune, and I will here cite a few distinguished individuals who have passed for good christians in other parts of the world, but who would be counted as heretics in the pious city of Mobile. I could add the names of Cuvier, Laplace, Herschell Bishop Brinkly, and a host of other names who have thrown open the field of science, but my design is not to write a book.

It may be said that none of these distinguished men have admitted the existence of species in the human race—granted—but they have admitted my other positions in Geology and Natural History, to which exceptions have been taken, and have always been ready to hear new facts or to investigate any scientific question

Rev William Buckland, D D, Canon of Christ Church, and Professor of Geology in the University of Oxford, says.

"If the suggestions I shall venture to propose, require some *modification* of the most commonly received and popular interpretation of the Mosaic narrative, this admission neither involves any impeachment of the authenticity of the text, nor of the judgment of those who have formerly interpreted it otherwise, *in the absence of information as to facts* which have but recently been brought to light, and if in this respect, geology should seem to require some little *concession* from the literal interpreter of scripture, it may be fairly held to afford ample compensation for this demand, by the large additions it has made to the evidences of natural religion, in a department where revelation was not designed to give information "

4*

"Some have attempted to ascribe the formation of all the stratified rocks to the effects of the Mosaic Deluge, an opinion which is irreconcilable with the enormous thickness and almost infinite subdivisions of the strata, and with the numerous and regular successions which they contain of the remains of animals and vegetables, differing more and more widely from existing species, as the strata in which we find them are placed at greater depths. The fact that a large portion of these remains belong to extinct genera, and almost all of them to extinct species, that lived and multiplied and died on or near the spots where they are now found, shows that the strata in which they occur were deposited slowly and gradually during long periods of time, and at widely distant intervals. These extinct animals and vegetables *could therefore have formed no part* of the *creation with which we are immediately connected.*"

"There is in truth (says Bishop Blomfield) no opposition or inconsistency between religion and science, commonly so called, except that which has been conjured up by injudicious zeal or false philosophy, mistaking the ends of divine revelation." "We may join the praises which are lavished upon philosophy and science, and fearlessly go forth with their votaries into all the various paths of research, by which the mind of man pierces into the hidden treasures of nature, and harmonizes its more conspicuous features and removes the veil which to the ignorant or careless observer, obscures the traces of God's glory in the works of his hands."

Dr Chalmers says "We conclude with adverting to the unanimity of Geologists in one point—the far superior antiquity of this globe to the commonly received date of it as taken from the writings of Moses What shall we think of this! we may feel a security as to those points in which they differ, but when they agree, this security fails There is no neutralization of authority among them as to the age of the world, and Cuvier with his catastrophes and epochs leaves the popular opinion nearly as far behind him, as they who trace our present continents upward through an indefinite series of ancestors, and assign many millions of years to the existence of each generation"

The following extracts are from John Pye Smith, D D F G. S one of the most learned commentators of England

"Ingenious calculations have been made of the capacity of the ark, as compared with the room requisite for the pairs of some animals, and the septuples of others; and it is remarkable that the well-intentioned calculators have formed their estimate upon a number of animals below the truth, to a degree which might appear incredible. They have usually satisfied themselves with a provision for three or four hundred species at most; as in general they show the most astonishing ignorance of every branch of Natural History. Of the existing mammalia (animals which nourish their young by breast) considerably more than one thousand species are known; of birds, fully five thousand; of Reptiles, very few kinds of which can live in water, two thousand, and the researches of travellers and naturalists are making frequent and most interesting additions to the number of these and all other classes. Of Insects (using the word in its popular sense) the number of species is immense, to say one hundred thousand would be moderate: each has its appropriate habitation and food, and these are necessary to its life, and the larger number could not live in water. Also the innumerable millions upon millions of animalcula must be provided for, for they have all their appropriate and diversified places and circumstances of existence. But all land animals have their geographical regions, to which their constitutional natures are congenial, and many could not live in any other situation. We cannot represent to ourselves the idea of their being brought into one small spot, from the polar regions, the torrid zone, and all other climates of Asia, Africa, Europe, America, Australia, and the thousands of islands, their preservation and provision, and the final disposal of them,—without bringing up the idea of miracles more stupendous than any that are recorded in Scripture, even what appear appalling in comparison. The great decisive miracle of Christianity, the RESURRECTION of the LORD JESUS,—sinks down before it.

"The persons of whom we are speaking have probably never apprehended any difficulty with respect to the inhabitants of the water, supposing that no provision was needed for their preservation. It may therefore be proper to notice some particulars. Such an additional quantity of water as their interpretation requires, would so dilute and alter the mass as to render it an unsuitable element for the existence of all the classes, and would kill or disperse their food; and all have their appropriate food. Many of the marine fishes and shell animals could not live in fresh water, and the fresh water ones would be destroyed by being kept even a short time in salt water. Some species can indeed live in brackish water, having been formed by their Creator to have their dwelling in estuaries and the portions of rivers approaching the sea: but even these would be affected, fatally in all probability, by the increased volume of water and the scattering and floating away of their nutriment.

"Thus, in a variety of ways, it is manifest that, upon the interpretation which I conceive to be erroneous, the preservation of animal life in the ark was immensely short of being adequate to what was necessary.

"Further; if we admit that interpretation, and also accede to the usual opinion that the Ararat upon which the ark rested was the celebrated mountain of that name in Armenia, and which tradition points out as being such,—we are involved in another perplexity. That mountain is nearly the height of our European Mont Blanc, and perpetual snow covers about five thousand feet from its summit. If the water rose, at its liquid temperature, so as to overflow that summit, the snows and icy masses would be melted, and, on the retiring of the flood, the exposed mountain would present its pinnacles and ridges, dreadful precipices of naked rock, adown which the four men and four women, and with hardly any exception the quadrupeds, would have found it utterly impossible to descend. To provide against this difficulty, to prevent them from being dashed to pieces,—must we again suppose a miracle? Must we conceive of the human beings and the animals, as transported through the air to the more level regions below, or that, by a miracle equally grand, they were enabled to glide unhurt down the wet and slippery faces of rock?

'One fact more I have to mention, in this range of argument There are trees of the most astonishing magnificence as to form and size, which grow, the one species in Africa, the other in the southern part of North America There are also methods of ascertaining the age of trees of the class to which they belong, with satisfaction generally, but with full evidence after they have passed the early stages of their growth. Individuals of these species now existing are proved, by those methods, to have begun to grow at an epoch long before the date of the deluge, if we even adopt the largest chronology that learned men have proposed. Had those trees been covered with water for three quarters of a year, they must have been destroyed; the most certain conditions of vegetable nature, for the class (the most perfect land plants) to which they belong, put such a result out of doubt. Here then we are met by another independant proof that the deluge did not extend to those regions of the earth.

"Such are the objections which present themselves against

the interpretation which, with grief I acknowledge, is generally admitted, in relation to the scriptural narrative of the deluge. It is a painful position in which I stand I seem to be taking the part of an enemy, adducing materials for skepticism, and doing nothing to remove them. But this situation for me is inseparable from the plan of these lectures, the only plan that appeared practicable. The apparent discrepancies, between the facts of science and the words of Scripture, must be *understood*, before we can make any attempt at their removal. I confide in the candour of my friends, that they will suspend their judgment till I am enabled to lay before them the way, in which I conceive that *independent* and *unforced* philological evidence will enable us satisfactorily to dispose of those difficulties "

"The actual Zoology and Botany of the earths surface exhibit several distinct regions, in each of which the indiginous animals and plants, are at least as to species and to a considerable amount as to genera, different from those of other Zoological and Botanical regions The habitation proper to one description of vegetable or animal families would be intolerable and speedily fatal to others" He goes on to argue that these *animals and plants were created where they are found*

"The earlier part of the book of Genesis consists of several distinct compositions, marked by their differences of style and by express formularies of commencement. It is entirely consonant with the idea of inspiration and established by the whole tenor of the Scriptural compositions, that the heavenly influence operated in a concurrence with the rational faculties of the inspired men; so that prophets and apostles wrote from their own knowledge and memory, the testimony of other portions, and written documents, to which indeed express appeal is often made From the evidence of language and of matter, we have no slight reasons for supposing that Moses compiled the chief facts of the book of Genesis, by arranging and connecting ancient memorials, under the divine direction, and probably during the middle part of his life which he spent in the retirements of Arabia."

Chrysostom lays down, as a principle for the interpretation of the beginning of Genesis, that Moses designed to write only of the sensible appearances of things, adapting both the matter and the expression to the capacities of the Israelites, a people recently delivered from the oppression of Egyptian slavery, and whose minds had not been elevated above low and common conceptions.

Dr Jennings and others entertain the same views respecting this book

---

"A most important subject of our inquiry is the genuine meaning of the word which we render *Earth* I assure my friends that I have not spared time or pains in pursuing this inquiry, and the result I briefly give. The most general sense of the word, is the portion of the universe which the Supreme Lord has assigned for the habitation of mankind When it is conjoined with "the heavens" it denotes the entire created world, but it is evident of itself that the practical understanding of the phrase would be in conformity with the ideas of the people who used it—frequently it stands for the Land of Palestine; and indeed for any country or district that is mentioned or referred to in the connexion Sometimes it denotes a mere plot of ground and sometimes the soil, clay and sand, or any earthy matter Often it is put figuratively for mankind, as the inhabitants of the world—considering all the evidence of the case. I can find no reason against our considering the word, subsequently to the first verse, and throughout the whole description of the six days, as designed to express *the part of the world which God was adapting for the dwelling of man and the animals connected with him* Of the spheroidal figure of the earth, *it is evident that the Hebrews had not the most distant conception* The passages which have been quoted, and many others abundantly convince me that I never entered into the purpose of Revelation to teach such geographical facts or any other kind of physical knowledge"

"I venture to think that man, as first created, and for many ages afterwards did not extend his race beyond certain limits, and therefore had no connexion with the extreme east The Indian and Pacific clusters of islands, Africa, Europe and America in which regions we have ocular demonstration that animals and vegetable creatures had existed, to a vast amount, uninterruptedly through periods past, of indescribable duration"

"There are declarations of Scripture which seem thus to oppose *facts* of which we have the same kind of sensible evidence that we have of the letters and words of the sacred volume and which we understand by the same intellectual faculties by which we apprehend the sense of that volume Now those appearances—facts I must call them—have been scrutinized with the utmost jealousy and rigour, and they stand impregnable their evidence is made brighter by every assault We must then turn to the other side of our research, we must admit the probability, that we have not rightly interpreted those portions of Scripture We must retrace our steps.'

———

"To those who have studied the phraseology of Scripture, there is no rule of interpretation more certain than this, that *universal terms* are often used to signify only a *very large* amount in number or quantity. The following passages, taken chiefly from the writings of Moses, will serve as instances 'And the famine was upon all the face of the earth—and all the earth came to Egypt, to buy from Joseph, for the famine was extreme in all the earth ' yet it is self-evident that only those countries are meant which lay within a practicable distance from Egypt, for the transport of so bulky an article as corn, carried, it is probable, on the backs of asses and camels ' All the cattle of Egypt died " yet the connection shows that this referred to some only, though no doubt very many, for, in subsequent parts of the same chapter, the cattle of the king and people of Egypt are mentioned in a way which shows that there were still remaining sufficient to constitute a considerable part of the nation's property —" He had smote every herb of the field and brake every tree of the field," but, a few days after, we find the devastation of the locusts thus described — "They did eat every herb of the land and all the fruit of the trees, which the hail had left "—' All the people brake off the golden ear-rings which were in their ears, and brought them unto Aaron ' me rung undoubtedly a large number of persons, but very far from being the whole, or even a majority, of the people as we may reasonably infer from the circumstance that the stroke of punitive justice for this act of idolatry, fell upon only three thousand persons, but the entire number of the Israelites at that time was a million and a half, and of them six hundred thousand were grown men trained to arms — "This day will I begin to put the terror of thee and the dread of thee upon the face of the nations under all the heavens " yet this declaration respects only the nations of Canaan and those lying upon its frontier, all being within a very small geographical district We likewise find the phrase, "under heaven," employed by the inspired writers to signify an extent of country, large indeed, but falling exceedingly short of a geographical universality. as, "I gave my heart to seek and search out by wisdom concerning all things that are done under heaven ——There were dwelling at Jerusalem, Jews, devout men, out of every nation under heaven " With this passage is combined a geographical enumeration, which points out the extent of country intended, as being from Italy to Persia, and from Egypt to the Black Sea and thus a probable elucidation is given to the declaration of the apostle, that "the gospel was preached to every creature which is under heaven."—"Ye shall be plucked from off the land whither thou goest to possess it, and the Lord shall scatter thee among all peoples, from one end of the earth even unto the other end of the earth." a phrophetic description of the dispersion of the Jewish people, as the punishment of their apostacy from God and rejection of the Messiah, but no one can regard the expression as denoting a proper geographical universality.—'The fame of David went forth into all the lands, [the plural of the word generally rendered *the earth*,] and Jehovah put the fear of him upon all the nations." This expression cannot be taken as reaching beyond the range of Syria, Armenia, Mesopotamia, Arabia, and Egypt.—'All the 'earth sought the presence of Solomon, to hear his wisdom.' This cannot be reasonably understood of any kind of resort but that of embassies and complimentary visits from sovereigns and states within such a distance, as might have appeared immense in those times, but which was small compared with even the then inhabited parts of the earth. The queen of Sheba was, we may think undoubtedly, the principal of these visitants. Our Lord himself condescended to use the style of the Jews in saying of her, that 'the queen of the south came from the uttermost parts of the earth to hear the wisdom of Solomon.' Yet her country was on either the Eastern or the Western side of the Arabian Gulf, about twelve or fourteen hundred miles south of Jerusalem, a mere trifle compared with the distances familiar to us in our days.

'Passages are numerous, in which the phrase "all the earth" signifies only the country of Palestine. In a few places it denotes the Chaldean empire; in one, that of Alexander.

'From these instances of the scriptural idiom in the application of phraseology similar to that in the narrative concerning the flood, I humbly think that those terms do not oblige us to understand a literal universality, so that we are exonerated from some otherwise insuperable difficulties in Natural History and Geology. If so much of the earth was overflowed as was occupied by the human race, both the physical and the moral ends of that awful visitation were answered.'

'The following extracts are valuable and interesting, as they show the impression made upon the mind of an able Bible critic, the elder Rosenmüller, at a time when geological researches were little known, and when Werner, at the age of 25, was but just beginning his career. He was far from the opinion which his son promulgated, fifteen years after, treading in the steps of Simplicius (in the sixth century) and Hetzel, Hase, and others in our own times, that Moses derived his history of the creation from the Egyptians. The resemblance is indeed remarkable, but I think it is much more rationally accounted for by supposing that the Egyptian and Phœnician traditions have flowed from a common source, the family of Noah, and that Moses, under the direction of divine inspiration, placed at the commencement of his great work the very written documents of primeval men which had descended in the Abrahamic line, and which were *the genuine records* whence the other traditions had been derived.—*J. P. Smith.*

"The enemies of religion act a very inequitable part when they require of us such explications of all chronological and historical difficulties, as should leave no portion of doubt remaining. Can it surprise any man that, in the most ancient of all writings, many things should be obscure to us, who live in times so extremely remote?—In consequence of the great advances which have been made in modern times, in Hebrew and Greek philology and the languages and antiquities of the east, no small number of dark and difficult passages have been satisfactorily elucidated, so as to make it perfectly clear that most objections have been engendered by ignorance. Every good writer must be presumed to speak according to the custom of the men among whom he lived, and their common use of language. I shall not meddle with the question whether the contents of the beginning of Genesis were by God revealed immediately to Moses, or that he derived them from more ancient records. The style, and the entire manner of the description, involve evidence of the highest antiquity. At every step we perceive proofs of that extreme simplicity which must have been the character of our race in its very infancy. With respect to divine subjects in particular, the first step of human knowledge must undoubtedly have consisted in conceptions of God derived from our own nature, ascribing to the Deity the same properties and perfections which men perceived in themselves, but in modes and degrees infinitely more perfect. Upon this principal are founded the representations of God which are given in the books of Moses, and many other parts of the Old Testament. Indeed this is, in my judgment, a very plain argument, not only of the genuineness and truth of those books, but of their DIVINE origin; seeing that they present to us a method of description concerning God and divine things, perfectly suited to the capacity of men in the earliest times, and yet the most sublime, and when truly understood can

5

dully interpreted, in perfect accordance with spiritual truth
The scoffers at revealed religion, philosophers as they please
to call themselves, betray an almost unpardonable ignorance,
when they make stumbling-blocks out of those constantly oc-
curring expressions of the Old Testament which speak of the
Deity [*anthropopathicis locutionibus*] in language borrowed
from human properties and actions. What can be a grosser
absurdity, and even folly than to require that Moses and the
prophets should have spoken of divine truths, in the very infancy of the human race, according to the philosophy of Des-
cartes, Newton, or Wolf?

"In the beginning God created this universe, the heavens
and the earth But, with respect to this earthly globe, it was
not at once the abode of men and animals, as it is now. but
there was a period during which it was utterly destitute of
such a furniture of things as it now possesses, it did not enjoy
the light of the sun, and it was completely covered with water,
Whether, at its first being brought into being, it possessed a
constitution like that of comets being consequently uninhab-
itable or whether it was reduced into its ruinal state, after a
vast space of time, by some kind of universal inundation of
water, with the concurrence of other causes both natural and
extraordinary cannot be with certainty determined from the
Mosaic narrative But this detracts nothing from the truth
and dignity of the narrative It never was in the mind or intention of Moses to unfold physical causes, of which he was
most probably ignorant, and which it was no part or object of
his divine commission to make known Nor could the Israelites for whose immediate benefit this history was intended,
have comprehended such matters for who can suppose that
they knew any thing of the nature of comets, or the planetary
constitution of the earth' J G Rosenmuller Antiquissima
Telluris Historia, a Mose Gen i° descripta, Ulm, 1776 pp 6
10, 11 12 71."

———

The learned and pious Bishop of Chester, says — ' Any curious information as to the structure of the earth ought still
less to be expected, by any one acquainted with the general
character of the Mosaic records. There is nothing in them
either to gratify the curiosity or *repress the researches* of mankind when brought, in the progress of cultivation, to calculate
the motions of the heavenly bodies or speculate on the formation of the globe The expressions of Moses are evidently *ac-
commodated* to the first and familiar notions derived from the
sensible appearances of the earth and heavens and the absurd

ity of supposing that the literal interpretation of terms in Scripture ought to *interfere with the advancement* of philosophical inquiry, would have been as generally forgotten as it once need, if the oppressors of Galileo had not found a place in history No rational naturalist would attempt to describe, either from the brief description in Genesis or otherwise, the process by which our system was brought from confusion into a regular and habitable state. No rational theologian will direct his hostility against any theory which, acknowledging the agency of the Creator, only attempts to point out the secondary instruments he has employed. '

———

The following extracts are from Sears' history of the Bible a work recommended by a large body of the Clergy of the U. States

' *No less than* 30,000 *various readings of the Old and New Testament have been discovered,* ' "and putting all alterations made knowingly, for the purpose of corrupting the text, out of the question, we *must admit,* that from the circumstances connected with transcribing, some *errata* may have found their way into it, and that the sacred Scriptures, have in this case suffered the same fate of other productions of antiquity"

He goes on to say, "that in the last 220 years, criticism has so much improved, and so many *new manuscripts* have come to light, as to call for a revision of the present authorized version, &c '

Now I presume that these errors do not implicate the great and important truths of the Bible, but here are abettors enough to throw open the field for a bold, presumptuous discussion on the Unity of the Human Race.

CPSIA information can be obtained
at www.ICGtesting.com
Printed in the USA
LVHW061523010522
717652LV00011B/358